Never Lonely Again

Never Lonely Again

Satisfying Your Soul With His Infinite Love

by

Malcolm Smith

HARRISON HOUSE

Tulsa, Oklahoma

06 05 04   10 9 8 7 6 5 4 3 2

Never Lonely Again
Satisfying Your Soul With His Infinite Love
ISBN 1-57794-618-9
(Formerly ISBN 1-880089-23-8)
Copyright © 2003 by Malcolm Smith
7986 Mainland Drive
San Antonio, TX 78250
www.malcolmsmith.org

Published by Harrison House, Inc.
P.O. Box 35035
Tulsa, Oklahoma 74137

Table of Contents

Preface vii

1   The Great Fracture 1

2   The Wilderness of Loneliness 13

3   The Pursuing Lover of Mankind 23

4   God Was With Joseph 35

5   Adventures With God 59

Epilogue 75

Preface

It was a cold, damp night in November, sometime in the early 1960s. A thin fog clung to the ground, and the wiper blades of the ancient Chevy groaned across the damp window. As we approached the outskirts of the town in Washington state, my hotel came into view, a dark silhouette against the background of a single streetlight.

The pastor of the little church where I had ministered that Thursday night thanked me again for the words I had shared with his congregation. The people were simple farm folk who had been overly appreciative, pumping my hand and thanking me for coming. Some of the older ladies had given me motherly hugs. It had been a long time since they had had a visiting speaker, especially one from England.

The hotel was cheap and long overdue for a total renovation—or better yet, demolition. The blinking light announcing vacancies spluttered against the wet darkness. A few cars were parked outside the ramshackle inn, and an orange glow, diffused in the fog, peered behind the curtains of one or two of the rooms. It was a forsaken, dismal sight.

The pastor again thanked me for coming and pressed the love offering into my hand. I guessed it to be pitifully small; after all, he didn't have the courage to give it to me in the light of his church office.

I slipped out of his car and trudged into the foyer where a surly night attendant scowled and grunted at me. I interpreted it as his way of saying, "Good night." The threadbare carpet was ingrained with the dirt from a thousand truckers whose boots had graced the hallways over the years. As I looked down the dimly lit hallway that led to my room, a nauseating feeling, to which I was becoming accustomed, swept over me. A dark wave of depression soon engulfed me.

My room was fourth on the left. The beige walls of the hall were dirty, and the brown paint was peeling off the doors. The thought that haunted me the most as I ambled toward the door was that no one was waiting for me in the room. Furthermore, after I closed and double-locked the door behind me, I wouldn't be expecting anyone either

In fact, apart from the pastor who was now pulling into his driveway where his wife and family waited for him in a bright, happy home, no one in the world knew where I was. If I died in my sleep in the creaky, uncomfortable bed, no one would know until the maid came to clean the room. I was alone and was making my way to my dungeon for the night.

Let me correct that statement. I was not only alone; I was lonely. And in these two words lies the difference between heaven and hell.

Loneliness is a pain-filled word that echoes through the empty caverns of our lives. When we use it, we are saying that something, or more correctly, *someone* is missing who ought to be there.

Man was not created to know loneliness. In fact, the word was not in his vocabulary until after the fracture between God and him occurred in the Garden of Eden. There, man was severed from his Creator by sin. Originally, he was created to have companionship with the God of the universe at the highest level.

Chapter 1

The Great Fracture

We discover who God is from the Scripture. The first revelation we receive of His character is that He is the primary Communicator. As God created the universe in Genesis 1, we see the words, "God said...," 12 times throughout the creation process.

On the sixth day of creation, God made Adam in His image and likeness. Of everything that goes into being made in the "image and likeness" of God, one of the primary similarities is that man talks. Adam and all of his progeny can communicate with each other in the same way God communicates. We can share our innermost thoughts and feelings with others through the words we speak.

Man communicates on the same wavelength, or level, as his Creator. When God spoke to Adam, an interpreter wasn't needed. Adam clearly understood Him. Today, anybody can talk to God in his or her native language.

In the Garden, the conversations between the man and deity were that of creature to Creator, of vice-regent of the earth to the Lord and Sovereign of creation.

The very essence of our existence is to communicate with the Creator: to listen to Him, understand what He is saying, and make an appropriate response to His requests. Furthermore, because the Creator is love, He created mankind to love and to be a partaker of that love. Man is capable of knowing God's love, delighting in it and reciprocating his love to God.

The love relationship enjoyed between the Creator and man was to be the foundation for all humankind. This relationship would reflect God's image on the earth. Knowing they were loved with an unconditional love, mankind was to demonstrate divine love in their behavior toward their fellow man.

Think about this: You and I were created to be the love companions of deity. We were to be His friends and the delight of His heart.

Through companionship and conversation with God, man would learn his true identity. He would know who he was, what his significance was in creation, and why he existed. He would know because His Creator told him so!

An inventor is a person who forms in his mind the reason for something's existence before he ever sets his hand to making it. After he has created his invention, he announces the reason for its existence and the way it should optimally function to achieve the end for which it was made.

God is the infinite inventor. Before the universe existed, He had a blueprint of creation in His mind. There was a reason for filling the solar systems with stars and planets and filling planet Earth with many different forms of life. He had a purpose in creating mankind.

When man was created in the Garden of Eden, he was introduced to his meaning for existence and his significance in the universe. Essentially, mankind was made to be God's friend and intimate companion. This meaning to man's life placed him on a plane infinitely higher than any other creature.

The friendship and communicated love between the Creator and man was a necessary part of man's existence. Only by living in that friendship would man function at his fullest potential.

Intimate Companions of God

The account in Genesis, which describes how mankind was created, underscores the fact that man was made for divine intimacy. God created all living things in twos, male and female. However, when He made the one who should be His friend, He made the two a one! The first human was male and female.

It was a strange sight in Eden. The monkey found companionship in the monkey. The parrot chatted to fellow parrots. The duck happily quacked with its mate in the reeds. All creation received a mate, but the one made in God's image had no other human in whom to find fulfillment.

By creating humankind as one person, unable to be fulfilled by another of his own kind, God was making it abundantly clear from where his fulfillment was to come. Man was created without a mate because at the heart of his existence, God was to be his mate, his first and ultimate friend. God and Adam talked, laughed, and played in the Garden of delight.

Adam did not know aloneness. He was satisfied in the friendship and love of the Creator. Adam never petitioned God for a mate. It was God who brought up the subject of his aloneness. He said, "...It is not good for the man to be alone; I will make him a helper suitable for him" (Gen. 2:18).

Having learned that God was his primary and deepest fulfillment, the time had come for Adam to discover the wonder and beauty of human companionship. God took a rib from Adam's side and built a body. He separated the female from the male and placed the female side of humanness in the newly created body.

It's only after we learn that we were made to be companions of God are we safe in developing relationships with other people.

God created mankind in order to find fulfillment for His deepest needs and longings. He also ordained a society of male and female companionship and commitment. Without the friendship with God, however, relationships with other people are sadly lacking, if not dysfunctional.

The Deceiver's Plan

Satan knew the only way he could gain control of mankind and achieve disorder and dysfunction in society was to fracture the relationship between God and man. He promptly marched into the Garden of Eden and introduced the foundational lie to the human race.

The deceiver usurped the position of the Inventor of mankind by presenting an alternate identity and meaning of life to the first couple. He accused God of lying and withholding from Adam and Eve their true significance. He enhanced his illusion with the words, "…you will be like God, knowing good and evil" (Gen. 3:5).

His lie essentially said, "Declare yourself independent from God. There is another life outside of being dependent on the Creator! In fact, outside of Him, you will discover that you have life in yourself. You will be a god and won't need Him."

Man pridefully rose and took the bait! In one deliberate act, he banished himself from his lover and friend. It was an act of rebellion with cosmic dimensions and ramifications. The creature owed his existence to the Creator and was supposed to yield his life back to Him. In one act of defiance, man snatched his life away from God in order to fulfill it himself.

Tragically, what had once been a life filled with joy and peace now burned in the ashes of separation from God. Man was now divorced from the only One for whom he was made and who alone could satisfy his inmost need for unconditional love and friendship.

Mankind's entire existence is held together by the voice of God. When this relationship was broken by sin, everything in his life began to disintegrate.

Man became separated and divided within himself. He lost his identity and the meaning to his existence. Soon, his relationships with his fellow man began to fracture as well.

Even though Adam and Eve intimately knew each other in the Garden, they were now suddenly alone. The definition for *alone* took on a new meaning. It no longer meant what it had when Adam was a solitary figure. For before the fracture, although he was alone, the presence of his Creator God was always with him.

A new word was now added to their vocabulary: *lonely,* a word that echoed emptiness and hurt throughout Adam and Eve's entire beings. *Lonely* meant "the pain of being deprived of something essential to life itself." It brought with it a deep sadness caused by the absence of God, who man intuitively knew should be there.

Without the conscious presence of God, man was lonely even while in the presence of others.

Without that voice telling him who he was and defining his worth and significance in the world, man would seek his identity and worth through other people. This caused him to perform in ways he believed would give him acceptance with others.

Without the Inventor to tell him who he was, man was at the mercy of every other voice in the world. He then began to believe what other people said about him.

Chapter 2

The Wilderness of Loneliness

Today, the agony of loneliness is one of man's greatest problems. It is the soil in which much of mankind's dysfunctional behavior grows and flourishes.

We are born lonely. From our earliest days, we try to fit in with others so that we will have people around us who like, affirm, and include us in their circles. We try extremely hard to be what others want us to be. So much so that we even allow those close to us to manipulate and dictate our everyday lives.

We allow ourselves to do things we do not want to do, even things that disgust us. We become mask wearers. We put on a different face for every occasion and try to portray ourselves in a way we believe our present company would like to see.

At other times, we take the position of manipulator and place other people in situations where they will need us, or where they will be forced to thank and appreciate us.

Sadly, behind the mask lies a lonely person who is confused by the multitude of voices that clamor to give him or her identity and meaning to life.

We run from marriage to marriage, always believing that the next partner will give us the fullness of life for which we are searching. We hope that the bottomless pit within us will be filled and our inner zoo of yearnings will be satisfied and silenced.

However, there is nobody on the planet who can fill our emptiness! We were created for the companionship of deity and were meant to be the friends of God. No mere creature can fill the emptiness when His presence is absent.

Lonely and Unwanted

I recently asked a number of people to tell me their worst fears, those terrifying thoughts that always lurk in the back of their minds. I was amazed to hear one after another relate how they will live with the fear that they will end up lonely and unwanted.

Many singles share the fear that they will never find a mate who will erase their loneliness. They fear they will die alone and be missed by no one. The words *spinster* and *bachelor* hang over them like dark clouds and pronounce the doom of years of emptiness.

Those who are married fear their mates will die before they do. Thus, they will be left alone with no one to love and care for them.

Perhaps the loneliest of all are the couples who "live together." Individually, they share the deep fear of the day when their partner will move on to someone else. They would be left alone to deal with the pain of rejection and loneliness.

Their live-in partner's refusal to commit to marriage silently gives them the message, "You are not worth marrying, just comfortable and convenient to live with at this present time!" After all, have you ever heard of a fiftieth anniversary of two people who have lived together?

The Sting of Loneliness

Most of us know what it's like to be lonely, even when we're in a crowded room. We are well familiar with the feeling that, although we speak the same language, we are effectively shut out of the lives of those who mill around us as if we were foreigners and spoke a strange tongue.

Many people are lonely in their marriages. Although they live in the same house and sleep in the same bed with their spouses, they still experience the continual, gnawing pain of loneliness. Their deepest desires have not been satisfied by their relationship with their marriage partner.

They have given up hope and live in the quiet hell of the empty abyss within.

There is also the heart-rending loneliness of those who have lost a loved one. Every night they come home to an empty house and sit alone at an empty table. They go to the familiar restaurant with the table by the window, the one that only needs one place setting.

Many of us have felt the rejection of someone who was of great importance to us, someone in whom we had put our hope, someone we thought would be the perfect friend and who would always be there.

Unfortunately, they let us down. They stabbed us in the back and betrayed us. We reeled at what they did, but the deeper hurt was their rejection of us. Along with that rejection came terrible waves of loneliness that flooded our inner being and left a heartache that no anesthesia could soothe.

When we walk through the darkest valleys of life and experience troubles that no one else can understand, when we numbly stare at tragedies in which our closest friends cannot relate, we know the pain of loneliness. When we have failed miserably, and those we thought were our best friends leave us as if we were leprous, the awful wilderness of loneliness has set in.

In order to combat loneliness, we fill our lives with all types of noise and amusement to drown out the echo of the pain in our hearts. We would rather listen to raucous noise than face the quiet agony of solitude.

At night, alone in the silence of darkness, we face the emptiness of our true inner selves. As a prison chaplain once told me, suicides take place after all the radios are silent.

Driven by Loneliness

Sometimes in desperation and sometimes with confidence, but always in ignorance, we return to the lie that we can find our fulfillment and completion in another person and not in God.

Single people ache for life partners who will bring them completion and fulfillment. Married people, bored and dissatisfied, believe that although it didn't work out on the first try, there is still time to find the perfect mate. "There must be a special somebody who will be my refuge and strength, my very present help in times of trouble!" they cry.

Mental health professionals tell us that everyone needs at least one friend: a close, intimate friend where they can be real and to whom they can expose their inmost self without the haunting fear that their worst secrets will one day be told to the world.

Some rare souls have a friend who fits that description. Ultimately though, no one person can be with us every time we find ourselves lonely and in need. The abyss of our hearts is so vast that no one can reach into our deepest recess and mend the loneliness. All of us need to be loved with an infinite and unconditional love, and no human on earth possesses such love.

Eventually, we despair of ever finding the satisfaction we are looking for in another person. The loneliness, however, remains. To anesthetize the inner pain, we turn away from people to the physical things of the earth—food, alcohol, and drugs. Others turn to sex, divorced from the committed love of marriage. They are satisfied with a depersonalized sex that, like drugs, only momentarily sedates us from the pain.

In our search for friendship and material pleasure, we are, whether we realize it or not, seeking after God who alone can satisfy.

The men who sneak into the brothel in search of love, the addicts who shoot their bodies full of heroine, and the drunks at the bar, are all unwittingly crying out for God. Even though they don't realize it, they want to be God's companion and friend. Every one of us will continually search in desperate frustration and restlessness until we come to rest in God.

Chapter 3

The Pursuing Lover
of Mankind

Man is not the only one who seeks companionship. Although God is complete in Himself, He *chose* to make man for Himself. He thus pursues us with infinite passion and patience.

In three different stories, Jesus describes God as the pursuing lover of mankind. He begins Luke 15 with the story of the shepherd who left 99 sheep in an open pasture to search for one lost sheep.

(vv. 4-7.) He searched for it because it was his sheep and made himself responsible to find it.

He then continues with the story of the woman who looked through every nook and cranny of her home to find one lost coin. (vv. 8-10.)

Finally, Jesus concludes with the powerful story of the prodigal son. (vv. 11-32.) He describes the father who scanned the horizon searching for the son who left home to waste his life. When he sees the young man from afar, his skeletal frame arrayed in rags and caked with pig filth, he runs to embrace him and smother him with kisses!

God wants to have our friendship back! Though He is complete in Himself, He chooses to need us and desires our fellowship.

One of the most heart-rending cries in Scripture is when God shares the agony of His heart over His rebellious people, Israel, centered in the northern tribe of Ephraim:

> How can I give you up, O Ephraim? How can I surrender you, O Israel?…My heart is turned over within Me, all my compassions are kindled.
>
> Hosea 11:8

Zephaniah, the prophet, described God:

> The Lord your God is in the midst of you, a Mighty One, a Savior [Who saves]! He will rejoice over you with joy; He will rest [in silent satisfaction] and in His love He will be silent and make no mention [of past sins, or even recall them]; He will exult over you with singing.
>
> Zephaniah 3:17 AMP

So often we only think about the needs and desires for which we petition God. From these examples, however, it is obvious that God has desires also. He wants our fellowship.

The psalmist cried, "As the deer pants for the water brooks, so my soul pants for Thee, O God" (Ps. 42:1). We could also translate this Scripture by showing God's infinite and unconditional love, "As the deer pants for the water brooks, so *My heart yearns for you, My child!*"

Words of Gentle Love

It was this love that caused God to approach Adam in the Garden of Eden immediately after he had declared his independence. God's first words to the rebellious man were words of gentle love.

It is an incredible story. God, who is in all places and immediately present to all persons, called into the Garden, "[Adam,] where are you?" (Gen. 3:9).

He could have squashed his life like an insect and start over again with a modified design, but He didn't! He pursued Adam and beckoned him to come out from his hiding place. He gave him the opportunity to admit his wrong and ask for pardon and restoration.

Unfortunately, Adam's response to God's question was nothing more than insolence and denial. And God responded to His arrogant creature by being the first to shed blood on the planet. He killed an animal and made clothing for the couple to cover their nakedness.

This was the beginning of a long parade of sacrifices that would end in the coming of God in the form of Jesus Christ. As the final and eternal sacrifice, Jesus shed His blood to purchase our complete pardon. He then offered us the clothing of His righteousness to cover our nakedness.

Adam's sin caused mankind to be banished from God's presence. This sin, however, did not keep God from pursuing man! Whenever anyone hears the voice of His love and turns toward God, He is there to pardon and restore the person to wholeness.

Steps Back to Friendship

As the human race began to multiply in the first centuries after the Fall, the ritualistic process of shedding the blood of substitutionary lambs began. Before Jesus died on the cross, this was their only way to be assured of God's salvation and love.

Through Abraham, God began to take steps toward His great plan of salvation. He needed to bring man back to the destiny from which sin had caused him to flee. God called Abraham to a covenant, which is the binding of two parties into union by a blood oath. When the covenant was completed, the Bible tells us Abraham was called "...the friend of God" (James 2:23).

God promised Abraham that He would give him a descendant who would bring about a covenant family of multiplied millions. Through this descendant, mankind would have the opportunity to be restored to friendship with God. That descendant was the Lord Jesus; and He told His disciples, the first ones who believed on Him, that they were His friends. (John 15:15.)

After Abraham, Moses built the tabernacle, or tent, in which the presence of God would dwell. Within its inner room, called the Holy of Holies, His presence and voice were made known. The Israelites lived in their tents around God's tent. Even though they were close by, they were still separated from His immediate presence by the walls of the tent. He only manifested His presence behind the curtain of the Holy of Holies.

At that time, only a few intimately knew Him. However, those few longed for the day when they would know Him in the fullness of His friendship. His presence was real to the psalmist, David. He often wrote in his psalms that he sang, clapped, and danced before the Lord as he worshiped Him. David raised his hands and prostrated himself before a God who was real and intensely personal. But even in such intimacy there was a cry for something closer in his relationship with God.

Solomon built a magnificent temple to replace the tent, and the nation of Israel built their homes in the land that surrounded the temple. God, however, desired that His presence would abide in the deepest recess of man's soul. That way, His presence would never have to leave him after he left the temple. He could depart from the temple and go to his own house in full awareness of that presence.

Immanuel Comes

The prophet Isaiah announced that a new thing was about to happen. God would make Himself known in a fashion hitherto unknown.

> Behold, a virgin will be with child and bear a son, and she will call His name Immanuel.
>
> Isaiah 7:14

The name *Immanuel* is Hebrew for "God with us." Jesus, born of the Virgin Mary, fulfilled the prophecy. He came to the earth in our humanity as our brother and walked among us.

The Creator sought our friendship and became a human. He could then speak directly to us. He took our place and died for us on the cross of Calvary; and through the Resurrection, He made it possible to forever have companionship with mankind.

For three years, the disciples walked the paths of Galilee and the streets of Jerusalem with Immanuel. They watched Him heal the sick and pardon the sinners. They sat and listened to Him teach for hours as He expounded on the meaning of life.

Then, the night before He died, Jesus told His disciples He was going away. He let them know that He was returning to His Father, the One who had sent Him. The disciples were stunned and confused. "Going away? No! It shall never be! How could we be left without the love, friendship, pardon, and healing we have known in Jesus?"

He further confused them by saying, "…it is to your advantage that I go away…" (John 16:7). How could anything be better than the living God in the person of Immanuel, Jesus the Christ, sitting across the table from them?

It was better because another One of the same kind and nature would come to take His place on earth, namely the Holy Spirit, the Helper. He would be the ultimate Immanuel, for He would be with us in a way that even Jesus could not accomplish.

The Holy Spirit would come upon us and live within our innermost being. He would never leave us because He would dwell in our bodies and minds, being spiritually married to our true selves.

The Holy Spirit is the One who is the Spirit of the Son of God and communicates to us the presence and power of Christ. He is the Spirit of the Father who assures us that we are His children.

He is truly the One for whom our whole being longs and yearns.

What David and other Old Testament saints sought so passionately as they lived under the Old Covenant becomes a reality to us through Jesus' shed blood and resurrection under the New Covenant. And what the pursuing lover of mankind lived, died, and rose from the dead for becomes His dream come true when we embrace Him and His redemptive work.

No longer must man meet his God in a certain structure in order to intimately communicate with Him. No longer must the Creator be separated from His beloved man. By the indwelling of the Holy Spirit, wherever a believer goes and whatever he does, he and his Creator are intimately joined together!

Chapter 4

God Was With Joseph

Joseph was one of the most remarkable men in the Bible. He demonstrated how to allow God to be with you in every trial and joy of life. He demonstrated many of the truths that would later be fully developed in the coming of the Lord Jesus.

Joseph was born lonely. When he was born, his brothers were old enough to be his father. As a result, he was never close to his brothers because of the age difference. It was a sad family in many respects. Jacob's children were born from four women; and mothers and children were constantly vying for first place in Jacob's affections.

Joseph was born to Rachel, Jacob's favorite wife. After his birth, the rest of the family knew that "first place" had been given to Joseph. Jacob continually doted on the little boy, almost to the exclusion of everyone else.

When Rachel bore her beloved husband their second son, Benjamin, she died during childbirth. Jacob grieved his much-loved wife for months. Alone and in despair, he retreated into his sorrow, which left Joseph all the more alone.

While he was growing up, Joseph spent time with his father and grandfather, Isaac, the son of Abraham. In the company of the pillars of Israel, he learned to read and write. The most important discourse he heard as he matured was how God had made a covenant with Abraham.

He could recite from memory how God told his great-grandfather, Abraham, to leave his country and travel to a foreign land. For his obedience, God promised Abraham that He would not only bless him, but He would also bless his descendants. Moreover, every family on earth would be blessed through Abraham. (Gen. 12:1-3.)

Joseph knew from an early age that he was part of this covenant, not because of anything he had done but because of his birthright. By incredible grace, he was born into a family who had a covenant with God. And it became part of his inheritance.

He learned how to walk in the blessing of God, knowing it was his by God's initiative and promise. He fulfilled the Word of God in that everyone with whom he came in contact was also blessed by the covenant.

Hatred Grows

Jacob's love for Joseph did not endear him to his brothers. Over the years their hatred increased as they jealously watched him walk closely with their father.

To make matters worse, God gave Joseph dreams about his future. Instead of quietly pondering the dreams, Joseph boldly told his family about them. Though thinly veiled in symbolism, Joseph told them they would one day give him the obeisance reserved only for ancient kings and lords of the earth.

Jacob later gave Joseph a "coat of many colors," which was something fathers usually presented to their firstborn. It was a sign upon the young man's shoulders that he was his father's favorite and was being groomed to become the head of the clan.

Joseph was his father's eyes and ears around the ranch. Even though he was very young, Jacob sent him to check on his brothers as they grazed the flocks near the city of Shechem. The brothers so deeply resented him that their hatred only needed an opportunity to turn to murder.

That opportunity came when they saw Joseph's coat billowing behind him as the jaunty young man came to check on them in the remote section of the grazing grounds.

They seized him and threw him into a dried-up well. All of the brothers wanted to kill him except Reuben who argued for his life. Finally, they sold him as a slave to passing traders who were on their way to Egypt.

Alone in Egypt

Put yourself in Joseph's shoes. He had been stripped of his dignity and rights and was forced to be a slave in Egypt. Any dream he may have once had of anyone bowing down to him seemed to be a fleeting memory. If he had felt loneliness among his brothers, he was alone in the land of the Egyptians.

Despite his downfall, he became successful in his new profession of slave and soon became the chief among slaves in the household of Potiphar. He answered to no one except his master. Nevertheless, he was still a slave. He was considered less than human in Potiphar's or any free man's eyes.

Potiphar had been made a eunuch in order to hold his position in the royal court and no longer had any sexual interest in his wife. With her physical needs being unmet, the desperately lonely woman made sexual advances toward the young slave.

In their household, she was of the highest rank next to Potiphar. She was not a slave girl from the kitchen, telling Joseph that she understood what he was going through and that she could take away his pain and loneliness. No, she was the wife of his owner, and she was telling him how handsome he was and that she wanted him!

Joseph was in his early twenties. He was a normal, healthy young man who was cut off from every friend he had ever known. He was faced with a situation where a prestigious and desirable woman was offering him a sexual relationship. Moreover, because of the positions they held, no one would ever know.

However, he refused her.

Apart from being a study in how a young man overcomes sexual temptation, this incident show us that even though Joseph was alone, he was not lonely. If he had been lonely, he would have been overwhelmed by the temptation and justified committing adultery with her.

The real temptation was more than glandular! This was not a test to see if he could overcome his sexual desires, but a test to see if the deepest needs of his spirit could be satisfied by another human being instead of God.

If we do not seek fellowship with God, we will seek companionship, acceptance, and love from people who will ultimately be unable to meet our needs. Only the eternal God is able to fill the inner void that overflows with needs too vast for any human to satisfy.

Alone, But Not Lonely

Joseph's secret is summed up in the phrase found throughout the Genesis account about his life, "The Lord was with Joseph." (Gen. 39:2,21,23.) God was with him and satisfied the deepest needs of his heart. His relationship with the Lord enabled him to be alone but not lonely.

Joseph's loneliness was swallowed up in the friendship and presence of God. He was so fulfilled by his relationship with God that the seductive presence of a beautiful, flattering female was no competition for the presence of God!

If he had been nursing the pain of rejection and loneliness, Joseph would have quickly succumbed to the embrace of this woman and become trapped in adultery. His divine friendship gave him a cool head and the strength to look at the situation with clarity and to walk away from a potentially sinful and destructive situation.

Joseph had learned the reality of the covenant from his father and grandfather. God had sworn by Himself to be with His people—as a nation, a family, and also individually. He promised to lovingly hold them in His hand.

Joseph's great-grandfather, Abraham, had been known as the "friend of God." (James 2:23.) Joseph had learned to covet and pursue that same kind of relationship with God, and his intimacy with God kept him from loneliness and harm.

Spirit and Soul Pain

Loneliness is a searing pain of the spirit and soul and can paralyze the mind and the body. It is the fear of being lost, like a child alone in a big city, with no one to hold his hand. Loneliness is the pain we feel when someone who is a vital ingredient to our life is missing. We feel as though we may die of spiritual malnutrition without him or her.

In the same way that Jesus knew the intimate presence of His Father, we can also know His presence through the Holy Spirit. Before His death, Jesus was rejected and deserted by his closest friends. As He approached the blackest hour of His life on earth, He said:

> Behold, an hour is coming, and has already come, for you to be scattered, each to his own home, and to leave Me alone; and yet I am not alone, because the Father is with Me.
>
> John 16:32

Even when He was alone, He did not experience loneliness. He was always conscious of His

Father's presence. We can also know that same warm presence regardless of the circumstances we may be experiencing.

Saved for Companionship

Modern evangelism often emphasizes that the purpose of salvation is to escape hell and go to heaven, often glossing over the fact that we are saved to be companions of God. The Holy Spirit is often defined as the anointing, the power or gifts, but seldom as the person of God who makes our friendship with our Creator a reality.

In the Acts of the Apostles, the Holy Spirit is said to "fall upon" certain individuals. (Acts 8:16.) This is an unfortunate translation, for in every other place in the New Testament, that word is translated as "embrace" or "hug."

The classic example is in Luke 15:20 where the father ran to the prodigal son and embraced him. The *King James Version* of the Bible translates it as "…fell on his neck, and kissed him."

The Holy Spirit falls on us in the same way. He divinely hugs us with a loving embrace, which causes us to know the reason for which we were born. This is the heart of the new covenant.

A Brazilian pastor told me about a time when he became very discouraged over the hardness of ministry and the lack of basic necessities that he had experienced while serving God. One day, he decided to quit the ministry. Before he did, however, he went to a quiet place and poured out his anger and resentment to God. He was furious that God had not kept His promises and supplied him with the grace he felt was lacking.

At this point in his story, he began to weep. He said, "As I angrily prayed, the voice of the Holy Spirit spoke loud and clear to my heart. He told me that if ministry was causing a rift between the two of us, then by all means I should quit. My friendship with God was far more important than all of the ministry I might perform for Him!"

As this dear pastor told me his story, I realized this was the heart of Christianity. We have made *success* to mean pastoring the largest church in the nation and winning more souls to the Lord than anyone else. However, these things fall short in comparison to becoming a friend of God. The Brazilian pastor returned to his ministry a new man. He is very successful today because he purposes to be a friend of God.

Joseph knew that friendship also. When he was faced with the temptation to sin, he was able to point to that presence from which he lived out

his life and say, "…How then could I do this great
evil, and sin against God?" (Gen. 39:9).

To say that God was with Joseph gave
powerful meaning to what looked like a meaningless existence. He did not need an affair with the
boss's wife. His existence was far from pointless.
God was his friend!

"God with us" does not refer to an impersonal,
uncaring eye that sees everything but does
nothing. Nor is He a weeping eye that sees what
is happening and says, "I'm sorry, I wish I could
help, but this is how life is!"

We must realize that in any painful or frus-
trating circumstance in which we find ourselves
God is actively, not passively, with us. He continually manifests His love, wisdom, and power to
us and causes His glory to become a reality in the
situations we face.

Mind Scripts

Part of our loneliness is because we have written a script in our minds of what life should be like and how people should treat us. Many erroneously understand faith to be the ability to control God! We believe that with enough faith He will create our script to our specifications and bring it to pass exactly as we have written it in our heads.

God does not order His Kingdom according to our suggestions but according to His plan. Faith responds to His goodness and rests in Him. It believes that He is at work in every situation, even when it feels as though our friends have left us and we are alone.

What does God do? Does He change the situation and cause the individuals involved to conform to our mental script? No, He makes the situation part of His plan.

Joseph summed this up when he said to his brothers many years later, "...you meant evil against me, but God meant it for good in order to bring about this present result, to preserve many people alive" (Gen. 50:20).

His brothers had written their script. They had intended life to turn out differently for their hated younger brother. They entitled their play "Frustrated Dreams" and employed the Ishmaelites as actors who would carry Joseph into Egypt and oblivion. Potiphar and his adulterous wife also became key players in their little drama.

The stage had been set to bury Joseph in Egypt. God, however, rewrote the script. He used all of the same actors, background scenery, and props. He just changed the ending! Utilizing an incredible twist in the plot, the script was rewritten as "Fulfilled Dreams"!

When we submit to God even in the situations where loneliness would win the day, we discover that the very designs of evil against us are turned to His glory and our good.

The book of Esther tells the account of Haman who sought to destroy all of the Jews because Mordecai, Queen Esther's beloved uncle, refused to bow down and worship him. At the suggestion of his wife, he had gallows built to hang his nemesis. (Est. 5:14.)

The night before the execution, however, King Ahasuerus could not sleep and asked that the book of memorable deeds to be brought to him, and he read of a time when Mordecai saved the king's life.

When the King learned that Mordecai had not been rewarded for his deed, by a quirky turn of fate, he looked to Haman to honor and exalt Mordecai. God once again rewrote the end of the script. The gallows in which Haman had prepared for Mordecai's execution ended up being the demise for his entire family and himself.

Proverbs 26:27 warns those who are digging a pit to beware lest they fall into it themselves.

It's God's Show

How do we submit to God as we sit in the empty rooms of life, angrily kicking the walls, wallowing in self-pity, and weeping in frustration because of our loneliness?

We must tear up our script—the one where we decided how life and people ought to treat us. We then place our life in the love, wisdom, and power of our Almighty Father and declare by faith that we will now live our lives on His stage and read lines from His book. In essence we become His slave. Becoming a slave of God, however, is not a bad thing, for it is only after we do this that we will truly be happy.

If Joseph had not placed His life in God's hands, he would have leaped at the opportunity to have an affair with Potiphar's wife. However, he did not see Potiphar as an enemy but as an instrument of God. He was one of God's actors, and Joseph told Potiphar's wife as much. To hurt Potiphar would have been to strike a blow at God.

Joseph recognized God's hand on his life. Because of this, he did not sulk in the corner and wait to die a bitter, old, lonely slave in a strange land. He embraced each situation he faced as though it was a part of God's plan to fulfill his destiny. He embraced the covenant that God gave Abraham and cashed in on it for Potiphar!

Potiphar was amazed at the prosperity of his business with Joseph at the helm. He did not purchase a sniveling man with a slave mentality but rather someone who knew that God takes the intentions of the wicked and turns them around for His glory. He saw a man who was not lonely but alive in the presence of God who promised to never leave him.

No wonder Joseph was promoted to the highest position in Potifer's household and no wonder Joseph refused to touch his wife. He was secure in his position in God. He was not lonely, just alone. He was not a pawn in the meaningless game of life. His God had worked out a plan and was using this woman's husband to be a part of it.

Joseph was a man who continued to believe in his dreams. Regardless of his circumstances, he never lost faith in his God-given dream and knew that one day God would exalt him. If he had doubted that the dream was truly from God, he never would have volunteered to interpret his fellow prisoners' dreams. Nor would he have interpreted Pharaoh's dream, which ultimately became the fulfillment of his own.

He was not a lonely, desperate victim who had been dealt a bad hand. It had never crossed his mind that the world owed him. He did not grab at anyone to see what he could get out of him or her to fill the emptiness of his lonely life.

It was evident through Joseph's words and actions that his life was in God's hands, and he was not about to fight against Him. He chose to trust that God would bring his dreams to pass.

In a word, Joseph was not lonely! He was a secure individual who was filled with faith and hope—not in the people around him or the circumstances in which he found himself—but in the Creator who had complete charge of his life.

Chapter 5

Adventures With God

God took the initiative to fill our lives with His presence and to satisfy our inner selves. Why then are so many believers lonely? Why was I so lonely every night in those motel rooms as I trekked from church to church?

It is interesting that at one time during those dark days, for some reason that I cannot now remember, I mentioned my loneliness and depression to a congregation. After the meeting, the dear people showered me with every form of over-the-counter medicine as well as prescription drugs to alleviate the darkness that attends loneliness.

Thanking them for their concern, I refused to take the mood-altering drugs. I assured them that I was in the middle of an adventure with God and would develop a relationship with Him that would enrich and mature my life. Ultimately, the experience gave me wonderful and precious treasures to share with others.

Through it all, I knew that the negative experiences of my loneliness would bring about something positive. Somehow, as I sat for hours in the mental and emotional darkness of those dingy, empty rooms, I believed I would discover God in a way I could not imagine.

Leaving the Dark Valley

The wisdom with which we live the Christian life is learned through the pressures of experience, where we are forced to take what we believe and make it uniquely our own. You are in the midst of an adventure with God. He wants His presence to manifest in your life in a manner that is beyond your wildest dreams at this moment.

In your heart, you know He is with you. It is through the experiences of life that the knowledge in your heart will make its way to your head. Once that happens, you will begin to think and look at life differently. You'll see life in the light of that truth.

Your loneliness is the dark valley in which you will find the reality of His presence. And in His strength you will be equipped to glorify Him in all of your relationships.

How do we do this? For me, it happened in a sequence of events over a period of months. Although I will explain it in a few paragraphs, this transformation was not a quick process. As you walk through your loneliness, please remember that I wrestled for weeks with some of the areas I am about to share with you.

First of all, I realized that I had been created to have a friendship with God. Being God's companion was my destiny. It's the reason I live and breathe. When I finally understood this, it was a life-changing revelation for me. I had thought that salvation simply meant that you went to heaven when you died, rather than becoming a friend of God while you were on the earth.

This revelation brought me to face and confess my sin of obsession with myself. Looking back, I realized that I had one passion in life, and that was to have others love, like, and affirm me. In that black valley, I prayed that God would give me the companionship and friends I so desperately wanted. I was searching for people who would satisfy all of my inner needs.

When I came to see that I was created to be the friend of God and that my goal as a born-again Christian should be to become His intimate partner, I realized how utterly selfish my prayers were. In effect, I had been ignoring the One who desired to fill my life with His love and friendship.

When I talked to God in prayer, I was obsessed with my script and myself. The reason I talked to Him in the first place was because I felt He was the One who could make my plan happen. In essence, I was asking the only One who truly loved me unconditionally and who alone could satisfy my inner longings to send people to love me instead.

I came to realize that part of my self-absorption was because I spent a lot of time envying other people's supposed happiness. I had an exaggerated perception of the bliss of others. I believed their lives were filled with continual joy, brought to them by loving friends and companions. Inevitably, this belief caused an exaggeration of my own misery, as well as a false perception of deprivation.

I had to confess all of this as the sin it was and yield it to the Cross. I then began to surrender all of the scripts I had written. Finally, I was willing to tear them up and accept His. I began to confess that He was the friend for whom I was looking.

I was determined to never again seek heart companionship in other people. God was doing a work in me and bringing me to a maturity I had been avoiding by hiding from Him in the noise and distraction of friendship.

One day, I knelt in a hotel and declared, "I accept this present loneliness as part of Your plan, and I now offer it to You. What do You want to do with it? What do You want to show me of Yourself so that I might be able to share it with others?"

A New Understanding

God's answer to me came through a totally new understanding of the person of the Holy Spirit. I realized how I had ignored Him, which sounded strange to my ears because I had come into contact with the reality of the Holy Spirit very early in my Christian life. However, I had always been so focused on the gifts of the Spirit and the never-ending search for His power in my life and ministry that I had completely ignored the Holy Spirit as a person.

I had never thought of Him as God on earth; Immanuel seeking to pour His love into me and to have a holy friendship with me.

It was while reading the account of the Holy Spirit "falling upon" the household of Cornelius in Acts 10:44 that I discovered that phrase. To my delight, it was speaking of the Spirit giving us a bear hug, embracing us with infinite, unconditional love.

When the Scripture says the Holy Spirit "fell upon" believers, it must be understood that He is giving us an embrace of love. It's a divine hug that imparts His love and life to us. The God who desires us meets us with an infinite bear hug, and we live in that embrace.

I repented of all the years I had ignored Him and then welcomed Him into the center of my life. My new desire and goal in life became to know God as my friend. I began to see how He was not only my life, but He was also the One who walks with me through my life. He not only fills the abyss within, but he also shares in the details of my life experiences.

I do not want you to think this was an orgy of feelings. There were moments of feeling and deep emotion, but for the most part, it was during my ordinary, everyday life when I did not necessarily *feel* His presence but confessed His faithfulness to stay by my side and help me, that I began to grow closer to Him.

He had said He would never leave me nor forsake me. (Heb. 13:5.) I learned to take His Word at face value. He was with me, which meant that in every hour of the day, I could count on the presence of the divine lover.

During that time, I first read this promise in the *Amplified Bible* and was stunned by God's emphatic promise of never leaving us:

> For He [God] Himself has said, I will not in any way fail you *nor* give you up *nor* leave you without support. [I will] not, [I will] not, [I will] not in any degree leave you helpless *nor* forsake *nor* let [you] down, (relax My hold on you)! [Assuredly not]
>
> Hebrews 13:5 AMP

Regardless of my feelings, I could be confident that He was with me at all times. When traveling, I might leave my wife behind, but He is with me. He indwells my body and will never leave me.

Believing that He was always with and in me took the form of a choice to abide in Him. I choose to be consciously present to Him, as opposed to choosing to be present to whatever form of darkness would seek to oppress me.

This deliberate choice of faith would put to death all of the sins associated with loneliness. Most importantly, it would put to death the subtle belief in the lie that said I could go through life independent of my Creator.

The awakening realization that I was not dealing with an impersonal power but with the person of God the Spirit drew me to listen to Him. I would sit back in my chair and invite Him to make known to me the love of God. Reading the Scripture, I recognized that the One who had inspired the original authors was in me to tell me what it meant.

I was moving away from being lonely and moving toward the fact that I was alone—I was absent from other people. God now filled the space that I once looked upon with horror as a wilderness of loneliness. It now became a place of solitude, a special time to talk with God and to build a friendship with Him.

Some people who read this may believe I became a recluse, or out of touch with the world. Quite the reverse happened! The wasted hours that were spent in self-pity were now transformed to see the world through His eyes. I felt my eyes being opened from a long blindness to see the needs of others and how I could be of use in their lives.

His love was not only for me to enjoy; but as it matured, He shared His love with others through me.

A Home for the Lonely

"But what about friends? I think I understand what you are saying about God being my friend, but I would like a few with skin on! Didn't God say it was not good for man to be alone?" The irate young woman almost shouted her words at me after a meeting where I shared these truths.

I reminded her that only after the meaning of life was discovered to be friendship with God did He bring about human companionship. We must tear up our agendas that outline who God brings across our path. Remember that as we commit our way to Him, He will direct our paths. (Prov. 3:6.)

When we look to people for the love and commitment that only God can give, we slowly destroy ourselves. We also destroy those from whom we are demanding what no human can give. Looking for perfect love in another person inevitably means we will leave behind a trail of relationships we have been a part of destroying!

We can come to a relationship with an awful void within us, a void that tries to suck the life out of those who join themselves to us. When they have nothing more to give, they drop out of our lives.

Some sense our presence approaching. They can feel the deadly suction of the vacuum within us. They flee before we can draw them into our web of emotional neediness and suck them dry.

On the other hand, coming to know God as our companion will greatly influence our lives. When we know the Spirit of God as our friend and that He brings us to a real unity with the Father and the Lord Jesus Christ, our deepest needs are met and we are no longer empty.

For the first time in our lives, we are free to really love people for who they are and not for how they can meet our needs or how they can be needed by us. We are secure in Jesus Christ. We will find people begin to come into our lives, sensing that they can safely receive love.

In the warmth of God's love and continuous presence, we are never lonely again!

Epilogue

Are you lonely? Are you ready to make the following faith choices in the light of what the Spirit of God has stirred in your heart as you have read this book?

Will you acknowledge that you never knew you were created to be God's intimate friend or that being the companion of deity is your destiny?

Are you ready to respond to the divine lover who has been seeking you all of your life and who desires to share Himself with you? If so, are you ready to confess that you have ignored Him who is Immanuel on the earth today, God the Holy Spirit?

Do you see how you have looked for the answer to your innermost needs in relationships and in any person who has passed through your life, demanding from them the unconditional love that only God can give?

As you face these important issues, do not be discouraged but know that the Lord is on your side. He died for you, was raised from the dead to bring you into His friendship, and He abundantly pardons you as you acknowledge your failings and sins.

You can come to Him now using your own words and welcoming Him into the center of your life. Begin a friendship with the triune God today through His Spirit, a precious relationship that will mature and deepen forever.

Prayer of Salvation

God loves you no matter who you are or what your past was like. He gave His one and only Son for you. The Bible tells us, "…whoever believes in him should not perish, but have eternal life" (John 3:16). Jesus laid down His life for mankind. He died, was buried and rose from the grave, so that we could spend eternity with Him in heaven and experience His best while we are living on the earth. If you would like to receive Jesus into your life, say the following prayer aloud and mean it from your heart.

Heavenly Father, I come to You admitting that I am a sinner. Right now, I choose to turn away from sin, and I ask You to cleanse me of all unrighteousness. I believe that Your Son, Jesus, died on the cross to take away my sins. I also believe that He rose from the dead so that I might be forgiven of my sins and be made righteous through faith in Him. I call on the name of Jesus Christ to be the Savior and Lord of my life. Jesus, I choose to follow You and ask that You fill me with the power of the Holy Spirit. I declare that I am a child of God. I am free from sin and am full of the righteousness of God. I am saved in Jesus' name. Amen.

If you prayed this prayer to receive Jesus Christ as your Savior for the first time, please contact us on our Web site at **www.harrisonhouse.com** to receive a free book.

Or you may write to us at:
Harrison House
P.O. Box 35035
Tulsa, Oklahoma 74153

About the Author

Malcolm Smith was born in London, England, and came to the United States in 1964. While the pastor of a church in Brooklyn, New York, his ministry was radi-  cally changed by the revelation that the heart of the gospel was founded in the unconditional love of God and expressed to mankind through Jesus Christ through the Abrahamic covenant. He became involved in the charismatic renewal in the sixties and seventies and was heard throughout the world on radio, TV, and through seminars and retreats. He is currently a bishop in the Community of the Holy Spirit. He and his wife, Nancy, head up the Zoe Community of the Holy Spirit in San Antonio, Texas. He conducts retreats and seminars as well as gives spiritual direction.

To contact Malcolm Smith
please write to:

Malcolm Smith
7986 Mainland Drive
San Antonio, TX 78250

Or visit him on the web at:
www.malcolmsmith.org

*Please include your prayer requests
and comments when you write.*

Other Books by Malcolm Smith

The Healing Heart of God

Forgiveness

Let God Love You

The Lost Secret of the New Covenant

Additional copies of this book
are available from your local bookstore.

If this book has been a blessing to you
or if you would like to see more of the
Harrison House product line,
please visit us on our Web site at
www.harrisonhouse.com

HARRISON HOUSE
Tulsa, Oklahoma 74153

The Harrison House Vision

Proclaiming the truth and the power

Of the Gospel of Jesus Christ

With excellence;

Challenging Christians to

Live victoriously,

Grow spiritually,

Know God intimately.